CAN YO

AND OTHER POEMS

Paul Ibell is a poet and author. He divides his time between England and the Continent, particularly Belgium and France. As a teenager, he lived for several years in Brussels, which remains one of his favourite cities.

His previous volume of poetry was *Passport* (Ardennes). He is also author of *Theatreland* (Bloomsbury), about London's past and present West End theatre scene, and of *Tennessee Williams* (Reaktion Books in the UK and University of Chicago Press in the USA) - a biography of America's greatest playwright, concentrating on the autobiographical element in his plays and poetry. Paul's first novel is *The Choice* (Ardennes), set in 1951, in London's Theatreland and in Brussels.

Paul's articles have appeared in a variety of magazines and newspapers, including *The Spectator*, *The New Statesman* and *The Evening Standard*.

CAN YOU SWIM?

AND OTHER POEMS

PAUL IBELL

To Vince and David,
love,
Paul
x
August '22

Ardennes

Published by Ardennes
27 Old Gloucester Street
London WC1N 3AX

First published 2021

Typeset by Born Group
Cover photograph © Mariell Amelie
Printed and bound in Great Britain by Clays Ltd, Elcograf S.p.A.

A catalogue for this book is available from the British Library.

ISBN 978-1-9998129-3-5

for Carol and Craig

Contents

Tu Sais Nager?

(Can you swim?)

Swimming a length of the local pool in Brussels,
aged fourteen,
I don't so much slice through the water as
crash through the chlorine,
a thrashing style that,
were I to replicate it in the Caribbean,
would attract the attention of any passing shark,
whose nerve endings would tell it
that a large wounded fish was flailing
in its death throes, so hurry up and
help it into eternity
before anyone else gets there first.

Fortunately I'm in Belgium
rather than the Bahamas,
so my movements (and I am
at least moving forward,
and on the surface,
however clumsily)
attract, instead, the
entirely benign interest of
a good-looking undergraduate,
working this summer holiday
as a lifeguard.

Leaving his chair,
he comes to the side of the pool,
crouches down and in

a kindly way
places his beautiful face as close to mine
as he can safely manage
without falling in,
so I can hear him over
the general background noise
as he asks me:
'Tu sais nager?'

'Oui!' I reply, trying to keep
the pool out of my mouth as I do so.
And, indeed, I could, but
over the years, as I have moved, often
inelegantly and erratically
through the waters of life,
I've sometimes thought of his
concern and how, if he'd seen
my journey from afar,
as a celestial lifeguard might,
he would several times have leant down
from the heavens and asked, solicitously,
'Tu sais nager?'

Taking Tennessee To The Coast

Whatever charms it may hold for others, Tennessee Williams strongly disliked St. Louis, Missouri, where he spent much of his early life. He was estranged from his father as a child and his mother as an adult. Despite his express request, verbally and in writing, that he be buried at sea, in the Gulf of Mexico, where the poet Hart Crane committed suicide by drowning, his brother had his body interred in a cemetery in St. Louis, next to their mother.

He'd have loved its audacity:
the poetry of the idea
and the exuberance
of the execution.

It took the tight-knit group
of daring strangers,
(whose kindness, they pledged,
he would be able to depend upon)
a long while to plan,
over suitably liquid lunches
and post-theatre dinners.

They consider themselves
a modern, American version of
the French Resistance:
in their case the French Quarter,
rising up, not against the Germans
but the unjustified imprisonment
of his body in the earth of a town
he'd spent his adult life
escaping from -

tunnelling out not with
an improvised tool, but
with his typewriter.

These *résistants*
are determined to liberate
him, to let him rest,
as he'd always intended and
often stated,
as close as possible
to the undersea grave
of his fellow poet Hart Crane.

And so, having taken Tennessee
from the ground before dawn,
they speed in the air
(the private plane a modern version
of Medici patronage,
albeit to a deceased artist)
all the way to the coast.

The yacht stands ready at the quay,
the crew, chosen for their looks,
a *tableau vivant* of Cocteau's sailors,
welcome the group on board,
before the skipper gives the order
to sail.

On a calm sea surface,
under a blazing blue sky
the spot is reached,
'We Have Not Long To Love'
recited, tears shed,

smiles shared, before
his coffin, adorned
with a flag bearing
not a national symbol
but quotes from his plays
and lines from his verse,
is pushed over the side
to the sound of cheers -
whoops of pleasure
such as might greet
the releasing
of a captive dolphin
back into the ocean.

The coffin,
embracing the metaphor,
bobs for a moment on the surface,
as if thanking them,
then joyfully slips beneath the
waves, the wild waters that
Tennessee had always loved
and where, at last,
he can leave behind the restlessness
of endless hotel rooms,
cruise liner cabins,
and an unwanted tomb,
to swim in the depths
of the eternal sea.

Brussels

Grand Place, teeming with tourists,
retains its gold-leafed charm,
the guild houses and glamorous
restaurants proclaiming the prosperity
of the European Union's capital city.

Half an hour to the south, on rolling
farmland overlooked by a vainglorious
monument made of earth and topped
by a lion, stands the site of the most
famous battle in history: Waterloo.

Here an earlier *grand projet*, Napoleon's
continental empire, died in a hail of musket
fire, artillery and the savage slashing
of cavalry sabres; an afternoon of carnage
that matched, in its bloody attrition
of young male flesh, the worst days
of the Somme.

Let the lesson at last be learned:
embrace a life of cafés among the
cobbled streets, the ancient squares
and art nouveau splendour of the
city of Bruegel and Jacques Brel.

Haute cuisine surpasses high politics;
chocolate, beer and waffles provide
more pleasure than any captured standards
or fallen fortresses - as Brussels knows.

Luisa Casati's Farewell

The Italian aristocrat, one of the richest and most elegantly flamboyant patrons of the arts of the early 20th century, owned the Venetian palace now home to the Peggy Guggenheim Collection. Her money long since gone after years of extravagance, she died in 1957, in a small flat in London, and was buried a few minutes' walk from Earl's Court tube station.

Her unique style, immortalised in numerous portraits, has continued to inspire fashion designers decades after her death, including John Galliano's 1998 collection for Christian Dior and, more recently, Alexander McQueen, as well as Karl Lagerfeld for Chanel...

The Marchesa's hearse is
passing through
the Knightsbridge streets,
watched by
moneyed matrons
for whom each new wrinkle,
sag, or sprinkling
of cellulite is the latest of
Death's heralds
to give notice
of their mortality.

She senses their shudders
at the sight of her coffin,
feeling a brief regret
at the contrast between today's
resentful reaction
and the (sometimes scandalised)
admiration that greeted

her appearance in her prime,
strolling down the most
fashionable streets and squares
of Venice, Paris and Rome,
kohled eyes blazing
beneath her flame-red hair,
a pair of cheetahs on a leash
clearing a path before her
as she paraded the latest
instalment in the artwork
that was her life.

A life of portraits by Boldini
and Augustus John,
photographs by Man Ray
and de Meyer,
dresses by Fortuny, Bakst and Worth,
dinners with Diaghilev
while writing him yet another cheque
for the Ballets Russes;
of parties whose extravagance
exhausted one of the
greatest fortunes in Europe,
until, a few fur coats
her only mementos
of what had been,
she ends her days
in a glorified bedsit
behind Harrods.

From there she is carried,
accompanied by mourners
who include her favourite

Venetian gondolier,
to her final rest, not in
San Michele or Père Lachaise,
but the spectacularly
inappropriate, bourgeois calm
of a grave underneath
a misspelt urn
in Brompton Cemetery,
whose daytime tedium
is disturbed, as darkness falls,
and to her amusement,
by the sexually-charged
choreography not of
Nijinsky's faun but of
leather-clad men rounding off
an evening in the gay bars
of Earl's Court...

Coming Home

When Covid-19 struck, the government offered to bring home every British citizen.

A dusty airfield, shimmering in the Middle Eastern sun.

A line of Britons, queuing,
in an orderly way, for the vast plane,
determined not to be left here, abroad,
a moment longer,
especially as this unique offer
from the government
came as such a surprise;
an opportunity none had dared
to hope for, given their circumstances.

But mainly, their parched throats
and dry, cracked lips are from the
punishing heat, the scorching rays
that hammered their heads,
as if trying to stop them.

Undeterred, they have made their way
together, long friendships renewed
as they crossed sand and scrubland
to the blazing tarmac,
leaving behind them the neat rows
of white-headstoned graves,
now empty as, after nearly eighty years,
the soldiers and airmen
at last come home.

On A Boat To Skye

Bonnie Prince Charlie's sea crossing to Skye has gone down in legend, immortalised on numerous shortbread biscuit tin covers and the haunting beauty of the Skye Boat Song. Though the Scots saw him as theirs, he was, to all intents and purposes, an Italian prince, having been born and bred in that country. Given this, and the failure of his cause, I imagine that on his escape across the water his heart would have belonged not to the Highlands but to the sunshine of the Mediterranean...

The oarsmen were doing their best,
he knew, but the splashes of water
were beginning to irritate him
as much as the bloody midges.

Being dressed as a woman while fleeing
the Duke of Cumberland's redcoats
was the least of the indignities he'd
endured since Culloden ended
all hopes of retaining his kingdom of Scotland,
let alone getting hold of England.

Still, it would make a good story,
shared over several bottles
with friends, once he was safely home.

Home. The fountains of Rome.
Warmth, sunlight, the incessant
but endearing sound of church bells,
the beauty of the people,
the many colours of their clothes,
their delight in *la bella figura*...

The girl, Flora, was nice enough.
Presentable rather than pretty,
but as for the rest of it,
the cold, the barren hills,
the endless freezing rain,
the dour Calvinism,
the fucking porridge,
he couldn't get away fast enough.

A French frigate was coming for him,
he'd learnt; the thought as tantalising
as that of the dishes he'd be served,
once he was back at his palazzo
and his wine cellar:
any battles fought not on the
cloying mud of Scottish hillsides
but in boozy recollection
in the course of long,
laughter-filled evenings,
the royal crest adorning
the porcelain of his dinner service
and the livery of his servants,
a world away from the
picturesque emptiness
of these outlying islands.

A sudden chill in the air jolts
him out of his dream and back
to the boat as another downpour
begins. Flora gives an apologetic,
encouraging smile, showing with
a gesture how he can most comfortably

wrap the unaccustomed female clothing
around him against the rain.

He follows her example then thanks her,
in the language whose very sound
he uses as an amulet against
the present and a prayer for the future:
Grazie, signorina. Grazie...

Diana

In Ovid's retelling of the Ancient Greek myth, Diana, goddess of hunting, was bathing in a woodland pool, attended by her female servants, when Actaeon, a young hunter, out with his dogs in pursuit of deer, accidentally stumbled across the scene and saw her naked. Outraged, the goddess transformed him into a stag. Actaeon was then torn to pieces by his own dogs...

She's long understood the price
that fame, celebrity, the semi-divine
glow that surrounds royalty,
demands of those who bathe in it.

To which must be added -
she concedes to a handful
of confidantes - the cost of having
flirted with the press, throwing
them information, photo-opportunities
and marital secrets
like one would throw chunks of meat
to hungry dogs.

She loves art and the stories,
the myths, that inspired so many
of the paintings that she's been
able to stand before, rapt,
in world-class galleries
opened privately, discreetly,
for her alone.

This was how she saw Titian's
Diana and Actaeon, in London,
the irony perfectly clear to her
of her namesake being the
goddess of hunting while she,
Diana, is the most sought-after
woman in the world.

Now, in Paris, as she walks through the
hotel's revolving door and out
into the night, the latest lover's
arm around her, partly to protect,
partly as if clutching his trophy,
the ultimate prize that her body represents,
she can't wait to get back
to the palace tomorrow morning,
to see her sons, to find
some shelter from the lenses
that have buzzed around her
like arrows from hunters' bows,
from the Riviera to the Ritz.

Determined to lose her pursuers,
the chauffeur slams his foot
on the accelerator.
The increased exhaust,
the smell of rubber burning
on the late-night Paris roads,
triggers an almost hormonal frenzy
among the paparazzi - just
as the mingled sweat and fear
of a stag serves only to excite the
following deerhounds,

urging them faster, their teeth bared,
saliva flying from their jaws
as they edge ever closer,
until the sudden slamming
of the Mercedes into an
underpass pillar
creates a shock wave
that shoots across the Channel
to rock the throne of England
and create a modern myth,
framed not in an art gallery
but in a million photographs:
Diana.

OCD

Water on the draining board.
Drops of it - like a liquid rash.
What stains will they cause?
His elbow aches at the thought
of the effort he'll need
to scrub and cleanse.

Have a cup of tea, he thinks.
A moment of calm.

Make sure, though,
to wash the cup
straight afterwards,
adding a drop of bleach,
to keep it pristine.

Then empty the kettle.
Completely.

Mustn't let limescale form.
It takes forever to get it off
and, once done, rinsing out
the kettle always leads to
drops of water on the draining board...

Bosie In Brighton

Lord Alfred Douglas (1870 to 1945), nicknamed Bosie, lived, in later life, in Hove. Here he is taking a winter walk along the seashore towards Brighton.

Ironic, he thinks
as he raises his collar
against the cold, his
shoes crunching on
the beach's pebbles,
that he should end his
days on the Sussex coast,
rather than the Lido in Venice
or a hotel in Dieppe.

Oscar's end was pitiful
but at least it was in Paris,
and with an audience.

He, however, finds himself
a lodger in a seaside town
past its best, stucco peeling,
in an England that's
bankrupt and rationed,
his life a mere footnote
to that of his long-dead
lover - to whom his
one immortal phrase,
'I am the Love that dare not
speak its name',
is invariably misattributed.

In his overcoat pocket
is a letter from a young poet,
an Oxford undergraduate who
has, to Bosie's astonishment,
read and enjoyed his verse.
Could he look at a sample of his
own, enclosed, and give him some advice?

Advice? He'd had a similar letter once,
from a teenage schoolboy
called Betjeman -
a foreign name, yet the
lad, precociously talented,
seemed to have a very
English sensibility.

He'd written back, encouraging
him to develop his youthful
experiments, polish his skill.

Youth!
The very word takes him back
to the 1890s, to the beauty
that he basked in every morning
in his shaving mirror.

These days the reflection is
closer to Oscar's horror-story
portrait in the attic:
every misdeed,
each unkindness,
all past rages,
carved on the old man's face

that he's been punished with.

He has no option but to
accept this delayed vengeance
for his teens and twenties,
but he can at least
hand on the torch,
the driving need to write:
the one thing
(apart from the love of a genius,
which must surely reflect some worth?)
that might redeem him.

The thought brings a smile
of satisfaction to his thin,
pale lips, while his back
straightens and his slumped
shoulders flex, defying
the chill of the sea breeze.
The pressure, as he turns,
is now behind him, harnessed
instead of fought against
as he heads back towards
the house, in his mind already
seated at the writing desk
having read the poems,
composing the letter
that he'll send
as one poet to another,
the winter sunshine
turning his iron-grey hair
gold again, the years
slipping from his face,

his lips once more red
and sensuous, as if eager
for a more exciting tongue
than his own to part them -
transported from Hove
back to Oxford,
rescued from life by art.

Brief Encounter

She could almost be Raine Spencer's ghost -
the mass of lacquered,
carefully sculpted hair
is what initially
draws my eyes from
the displays in Bond Street windows
to focus on this eighty-something
Mayfair matron.

There's nothing sparkly about her,
though she has the almost obligatory pearls
for a woman of her age and class.

Hanging from her stick-thin
yet immaculately-clad arm
(a tailored velvet jacket)
is a bag from some
expensive store or other.

But who is this look,
this costly - in terms of
time and effort,
as much as cash -
ensemble for?

At first her face seems
to offer no clues,
but then I wonder if its very blankness
suggests some answers.

Is the layer of make-up
a defence against age, as
Hamlet's graveside speech
might suggest, and may
the taut mask she presents
be created not by Botox,
but by her own rigid fixing
of facial muscles:
a long-practised act of will?

May it, in any case,
represent not misplaced vanity,
but a shield against an
incomprehensible and
often hostile world?
Or, more engagingly,
(though engagement is exactly
what it's designed to rebuff)
a positive display of resistance -
a pre-emptive strike
against 21st century life?

If so, it has the opposite effect on me,
as it makes me wonder
what mind hides
behind the face,
what heart beats beneath
the couture.

Unable to ask,
I imagine the life she leads:
the many-roomed flat
too big for her since

her husband died.

No children.
They'd tried,
but it seemed that...
She didn't like to dwell on it.
That's not how she'd been brought up.

Her few friends have gone too,
her regular points of contact
with the world
now reduced to her hairdresser
and her priest.

The England she knew -
the map an imperial red;
her older brother dashing
in his pilot's uniform
before being killed over Germany;
debutantes presented at Court;
tea dances and crooners -
has vanished.

She knows she no longer belongs,
that even in Mayfair she's a
relic, a moving museum piece,
but she carries on.

Why?
Because Mummy
would have wanted her to.
God's part of the equation,
of course, what with suicide being a sin

24

and the hope of something better ahead
when she finally sighs her last.

But it's for Mummy, really,
that she forces herself out of bed
every morning,
running the bath and beginning
the same pointless but perfectly-groomed
routine - a dutiful observation
of standards.

Yet now, for once, as she heads down
Bond Street towards Piccadilly
for afternoon tea at Fortnum's,
she notices a man
actually looking at her
with, she's astonished to register,
a sympathetic enquiry
in his eyes.

This recognition of her existence
gives her an unexpected and
all-too-rare lift,
providing a stronger pleasure,
a warmer glow than
the brief, unspoken contact
really warrants,
so, throwing habit to the winds
(along with Mummy's rules),
she makes both our days
by turning her head, ever so slightly,
towards me and smiling.

Orpheus On The Underground

*When this was written tube trains were still packed every rush hour and
people worked in offices rather than at home...*

The tube's like an outtake from Hades.
A carriage-full of wraiths;
mere echoes of life,
whose dreams died as they
descended to the Piccadilly line.

Seated near the door
but wedged between two
manspreading commuters,
is a would-be lifeguard
haunted by her last holiday
on an Australian beach.

Standing, stiffly, is a guy whose football career
foundered at eighteen with a knee injury,
his legs destined to be trapped under
a City desk,
instead of charging down a
playing field
to spectators' cheers.

A little further along the carriage,
with its straps like remaindered
bondage gear
hanging limply above the soul-scuffed floor,
a woman wears a camera
like a badge of office.

26

Is she a tourist?
A photojournalist?
Or do her clothes - sky-blue,
as if in mockery of where we are,
and topped with a cheekily scarlet scarf -
suggest a more artistic, theatrical life
behind the lens?

The train pulls into the station,
where the platform prisoners
clutch their mobiles
as if to signal to
their uninterested (indeed oblivious)
neighbours that they, the phone-wielders,
are not yet among the permanently dead,
but still have some link
to life above ground.

Escaping through the opening doors
we rush through the tunnels before us,
yearning for fresh air,
while a busker
promises a way out and upwards
as he sings of the streets of London.
Don't walk up the escalators - run!
Yes! You're almost there!

Nearly out!
But remember, as the ancient
Orpheus fatally forgot,
with freedom
tantalisingly close,
you mustn't, mustn't look back...

Speak!

(Since everyone else is doing rap these days…)

Used to be that people spoke -
now it seems that habit's broke!
What's this stuff with phones all day?
That's not the way to be, I say!

If you have a friend don't sit and send
some text or link; *tell* them what you think!
So much staring at a screen!
It drives me to the brink
- like piles of dishes in the sink!
Things really should be better.
We need a *new* trendsetter.
Time to make a different choice.
Time for you to use your voice!

Speak! What's happ'ning in your life?
You cool? You chilled? Or facing strife?
Either way, I say, it's so much better
to say the word, not text the letter.

People used to meet, to smile and greet,
share a meal, share a sofa,
be a doer, not a loafer,
talk about the day they'd had - was it good or was it bad?
Did they like that evening's food?
Now you have to *guess* their mood
'Cause they're staring at their phone -
Can't they leave the thing alone?

Why not put machines away?
See if you can save the day -
be the star in your own play!
For humanity and grace people should be face to face.
Like? Want?
No trick.
Don't click.
Don't swipe, don't type. You're human. Speak!
So much better. Perfect! Peak!
Speak!

A Bad Hair Day

Marylebone, London

Sitting at an inside restaurant window seat,
it being too cold for pavement café culture today,
I glance up from my coffee cup to see
a woman, in a doorway, staring at me.

There's nothing inquisitive about her look,
no hint of interest, let alone flirtation.
Indeed, it's unsettlingly harsh,
determined, challenging;
striking a strange, discordant note
among the *chic* shops and designer pubs
that cluster in the picturesque alleys,
squares and mews of this part of London.

I look down, concentrating on the
coffee cup's branding of Lavazza -
its contents dark and welcome,
warm; its name alone
enough to conjure up the conviviality
of a Roman bar or the astronomically-priced
elegance of a café on the Piazza San Marco.

Some time later, my mind back with a bump
in London, I get up to leave, only to see
through the window as I walk towards the door
that the woman is still there,
the direction and cold intensity
of her eyes unchanged.

Christ knows what this is about,
but then, I wonder, turning bemused irritation
into fantasy, perhaps she represents something
long before the Christian era –
a myth belonging to dark Aegean hillsides
somehow transported through time, over
mountains and seas, to present-day England.

The thought proves prescient, for,
as I make my way out,
into the street,
from the corner of my eye
(like Perseus, I feel it wiser to view her indirectly)
I see not only the stony set of her face,
but that her shaggy grey-blonde hair
parts involuntarily in several places,
as little dark-scaled snakes,
embodiments of the poison
chilling her non-human veins,
emerge, writhing, their fangs bared
as they hiss impotently
against the clatter of my Chelsea boots' heels
striking the pavement as I stride
beyond their reach: for
their mistress, the Medusa of Marylebone Lane,
is rooted to the spot – as stuck fast
in her doorway as a statue in its niche;
as if she, having stared too long at me,
caught her own reflection in the
restaurant window and,
in an inadvertently suicidal act,
has turned herself to stone.

Forty Years On

(for Stuart)

Forty Years On is Harrow's best-known school song. In the late 1960s Alan Bennett wrote a play, set in a public school, with the same title. It seems an appropriate one for this poem...

Though forty years have passed,
the voice at the end of the telephone
remains the same - unwearied
by age, a velvety strength
still implicit in its tones,
the allusions and enthusiasms
of his conversation still
those of a scholar,
though no longer those
of the Headmaster
he once was.

I was sixteen when we met,
allocated to sit next to his wife
(an understatedly glamorous
figure, with a South African accent
that spoke, to my romanticised view
of the world, of the vineyards
of the Cape, of the endless veldt,
of Rorke's Drift and the Zulu wars)
when they came to my boarding house
for one of the first dinners
they attended after the school
was placed in his hands.

The friendship that was seeded
that evening took shape
in the years after I left,
as I, like he had years before,
became an author - a deeper
and more nourishing
link than shared
memories of chapel services,
his lectures in the school theatre,
and the neighbourliness
of watching the First XV
thundering towards the
rugby pitch's twilight goal
on winter afternoons.

Finishing the call,
the feeling is always the same:
the half-hidden
sense that, whenever
I hear him speak,
part of me will always
be a sixteen year-old
schoolboy, safe
from the pressures
and perils of the adult world,
yet with all the potential
that it offers still ahead,
having - unusually,
reassuringly, excitingly -
his Headmaster as
an unexpected ally and
future friend.

On The Beach

The South of France, mid 1950s.

A holiday afternoon.
The sand beneath his bare feet
as he carries his eldest child,
his boy, laughing on his shoulders,
from the cooling sea back to
the June heat of a Mediterranean beach
where his wife, in a straw hat and polka-dot dress,
has prepared a picnic, with the twin girls
by her side, making sandcastles.

It was for moments like this that he'd struggled,
his army boots heavy with water,
out of the sea once before,
to be met, not by ice cream vans
but by bullet-spraying pill boxes,
until they were shattered into flame-filled ruins
by the heavy guns of the British fleet,
its vast warships providing a hail of
artillery shells to pummel the German positions
- as their land-locked cousins had done
at the Somme and Passchendaele for his father,
nearly thirty years before.

For a brief moment the idea of his boy
facing a third German war clouds his thoughts,
but he quickly dismisses them to the same place
that he keeps memories of his best friend's
chest exploding in blood and shrapnel

outside Caen, and his sergeant's joke
cut short by a sniper's bullet less than
a month before the longed-for peace.

Peace, he reminds himself,
is what he fought for
and he owes it to himself,
his lost comrades and his family
to enjoy it. To live not in the past,
but right now,
facing the future.

'Come on, Darling!' she shouts.

His heart full, he grins at her, takes the boy
from his shoulders then races him
up the beach, a joyful form of the freedom
won though his harder, darker arrival in
Normandy, in '44.

I Have

I have hung on a cross for you.

I have written on the walls of Babylon
and on tablets of stone.
I have stood in Greek temples -
a bronze statue wielding a thunderbolt.

I have left a princely throne,
to show a path to enlightenment;
spoken through shamans
from the Steppes to the Great Plains.

I have done all this for you,
yet your universal reaction,
from Acropolis to Amazon,
from cave to cathedral,
has been one of terror:
your focus not on the
life I have given you,
but fear of what follows.

When will you learn
that, shining through
every incarnation,
all I have ever asked,
and the sum of what
I have always offered
are exactly the same?
Nothing more complicated
nor less joyful than love.

The Last Emperor

Romulus Augustulus (ie 'little Augustus') was the 16 year-old last Emperor of Rome, ruling over the remains of the Western Roman Empire after being placed on the throne by his father, a general. He ruled for less than a year before being deposed, on 4th September 476, by the German soldier Odoacer, who gave himself the new title of King of Italy. This is the traditional date for the end of Ancient Rome and the beginning of the Dark Ages. Unlike most previous emperors, the boy's life was spared when he was overthrown - allegedly because of his youth and beauty. He left the palace and was never heard of again...

Ravenna, September 476.

He had known the empire now extended
no further than a week's march
from the palace, but had accepted
the crown when his father placed
the golden laurels on his head.

What teenager wouldn't want
to outrank his tutors? Which
red-blooded boy would not want
a room full of slave girls
at his disposal?

What sets him apart from his
predecessors, however, is
his total lack of interest in power,
even had real power been available.
No, what he wants, like Nero

centuries before him, is to be
accepted as an artist. And what better
platform for his poems, his plays?

He has made real headway
with both in the months
since he ascended the throne,
dining with actors and producers,
publishers and editors. They flatter
him, of course, claiming that, under him,
Ravenna, the capital since the
old one had been abandoned as too
vulnerable to barbarian incursions,
now outshines the ancient city.
That the elegance of his person
matches the sophistication
of his court.

It has been a conscious decision to
leave less elevated matters to
his father, so the last hour of this
fateful morning has been spent,
not studying the increasingly
precarious military situation, but
discussing, with his Master of Ceremonies,
the seating plan for that evening's recital.

He's been used, in recent days,
to the noise of barked commands,
of soldiers running, of trumpets
summoning them to beat off the
latest attack on the outskirts of the city,
so it's not until the last moment

that he realises something is
more than usually wrong.

This time the shouts have been louder,
more intense, but it's the following
quiet, the absence of the many servants,
the lack of the sound of spears being slapped
into a salute as the bodyguards change
shift outside the doors to his private quarters,
that finally warns him.

'Majesty!' Not so much a cry as a scream,
as his favourite tailor bursts through the
doors, propelled forward by a spear
slamming into his back, the blood
pumping out through his now-silenced
throat, as he thrashes around on the floor
before dying at his feet.

He bends to touch the man's head
as another, this time his father's,
rolls along the marble floor towards him,
followed by a crush of barbarian soldiers
who swarm through the doors to
secure the room, covering all exits,
before their leader, the German general
Odoacer, strides in.

Romulus finds, at the moment of his death,
an unexpected courage - unlike the
Master of Ceremonies who cowers,
whimpering, behind the table on which
so many entertainments have been planned.

'General! You have my empire.
May I have your sword?
I should like to die as a Roman,
and I find myself with no sword to fall upon.'

The German is not known as a man of pity,
but he has heard of this little emperor,
of his poems and his theatre, his concerts.
Odoacer kills for profit, not pleasure,
so, faced with the slim youth
in person, more Adonis than Augustus,
he decides to treat him not as
a rival, but a unique opportunity.
A chance to appease the gods by seizing
a kingdom through an act of mercy.

To his followers' astonishment, the
automatic hardness of his expression
softens and he speaks, in formal
Latin, with barely a trace of his
harsh northern accent.

'Boy, you were not made to wield a sword,
but to write a sonnet. A safer occupation
than trying to hold on to a throne.
These men' - he points to a pair of soldiers
standing near him, their own
swords drawn and ready -
'will accompany you as you collect
whatever you can carry with you,
then see you safely to the city gates.
If you're the artist your courtiers claim,

you'll make a living. Far from Ravenna,
if you value your life.'

An hour later, Romulus, the last Roman,
named after the very first, shakes the hands
of the soldiers who have escorted him
just beyond the city wall and set him on
his way along the tree-lined road that
leads south towards Campania. There's
a villa there, owned by an actor he has
corresponded with about the latest trends
in theatre. Somewhere he can stay as he
starts his new career.

Slung over his shoulder, on top of the
fashionable cloak that is the sole clue
to his previous status, is a small travel bag
containing gold coins, a handful of diamonds,
some food for the journey - and a stash of manuscripts.
Best of all, safely wrapped in a silk scarf, is
something of more use to his new position
than any sword could ever be: a conduit
for his thoughts and the means to earn a
future living - his favourite pen.

No Joke!

The call was the usual one,
a light-hearted chat on his way home
from the hospital, this time his voice
interrupted and overborne
by a dog's rapid barking.

'I wish I'd got that revolver
you wave around!' he quipped,
referring to my jokey reference
to blazing away with one
at the usual suspects - bad drivers,
aggressive cyclists, unhelpful
shop assistants...

It wasn't so funny when the SWAT team
exploded the suburban calm
of the house where I was staying,
bursting through the front door
before my 90 year-old aunt
had a chance to open it and
offer them the tea and biscuits
that she was convinced anyone
in a uniform deserved.

She saw the funny side, eventually,
once the guest bedroom was put back
in order and my friend had given
a statement under oath that
he'd been joking.

As the coppers headed back to their cars,
my aunt gave me a conspiratorial wink.

'Thank goodness they didn't look
for your grandfather's little souvenir!'
she smiled, pulling from under a tea cosy
the Luger that he'd taken from a
German officer at the end of the war.

'I never could get the hang of the
safety catch', she sighed, pulling the trigger
and sending an astonishingly noisy bullet
into one of the porcelain figurines
on the mantlepiece, shattering it
into a hundred pieces.

How we laughed!

Then we heard the heavy shoes
pounding back up the drive, followed by
an insistent ringing of the doorbell.

'I'd better put the kettle on again, dear', she said.

In The Morning

He wakes up every morning first;
each day it's just the same.
Before his eyes are opened,
he wants to speak her name,
to softly stroke her lustrous hair.

But it isn't she who's lying there,
his long-lost lover, tousled, bare.
For this is now, he's middle aged
and 'settled', 'safe', adequately waged,
with a thicker waist, lines on his face
and a different woman, who he wed,
shares the sexless marriage bed,
the usurper of his true love's place.

He gets up, dons his dressing gown,
puts on his slippers, then heads down
to prepare the frugal breakfast tray.
The ritual is the same each day.
And as the kettle starts to boil
he smells *her* cooking, olive oil,
exotic dishes she produced
when - as with sex - she introduced
his teenage self, gap-yeared away
to Italy, and heard her say,
between their kisses: 'I love you! I do!
English boy, do you love me too?'

Three months it lasted. She said she'd write
but didn't, nor phoned; now every night

they're on the beach, or in her bed,
and after sex she lays her head
upon his chest - then his heart breaks
at realising, when he wakes,
it'll never be, what he wants most,
and so he butters Mary's toast
then climbs the stairs, gives her the tray,
and starts another half-lived day.

Images In The Fireplace Flames

On a chilly late afternoon, snug indoors, we can let our
imaginations roam as we look into the flames in a fireplace.
But what dreams does it have?

I've been keeping people warm
for a hundred and fifty years,
families sitting beside me
after Sunday lunch,
relaxed and cosy as
the rain throws itself
at the window panes
in a doomed attempt to join them.

All very restful,
and I'm delighted to oblige,
especially when people stare
into my flames,
conjuring not only faces
and figures
in the dancing red and gold,
but other lives,
fresher lovers.

Well, I have dreams, too!
When lit by old newspapers,
kindling sticks and coal
(or, when the family's showing off,
with sustainably-sourced logs)
I transport myself

from this comfortable
domestic setting.

Sometimes I'm a blazing beacon,
in a metal nest high on a wooden pole,
warning an older England of the
approaching Spanish Armada.

At others, less dramatically,
I warm an invalid's bedroom
as they recover, cheered by
my glowing coals.

I'm not alone in these dreams,
but the flame community,
as it were, contains as
wide a range of types,
and - ironically -
shades of darkness,
as anything human.

There are, among us, delinquents
who dream of erupting
when petrol bombs find their targets,
or searing war-scarred streets
as car bombs explode.

Fanatics, who long to recreate
the terror of the Inquisition,
to replay the death of Joan of Arc,
in funeral pyres stretching from
Spain to Smithfield.

My own religion is gentle,
my flames not
instruments of punishment
but the small, subtle,
yet unquenchable
flickering of candles in
churches, lights that
lighten the darkness
as gentle prayers rise
unobtrusively to heaven.

Not that I'm a prude,
you understand.
I have my needs,
my desires,
like anyone else,
and I've more than once
imagined myself as
the heat in front of which a
Hollywood starlet lies,
seductively, on a rug.

Similarly, though old, I can still
create my own updraft with
thoughts of devouring the
ripely lush figure
of Ursula Andress
as the immortal queen,
bathed in fire in *She,*
while one of my few
professional regrets is
passing on the chance

to be an extra in
The Towering Inferno.

But mostly, when I dream,
it's of calmer scenes:
Christmas lunches,
après-ski drinks,
winter pubs after long
country walks,
or a pre-war
miner's kitchen
where he soaks
in front of me after
sluicing off the worst
of the coal under
a tap in the back yard.

I have no fear of death,
for I've been resurrected
so often - every time
I'm lit - that I know
I'll never fully die.
And if I do,
the flames of Hell can hold
no fear for me, while
those of Heaven will
welcome me with a
brighter, purer light
than anything I
can manage here...

Second Childhood

Ring a ring of roses, we sang
as children in the playground;
the place where we ran and laughed,
fought, burned off our energy.

Now, those days mere memories,
for those who still retain them,
we're silent apart from occasional
muttering; not holding hands in a ring,
but slumped in a semi-circle of the elderly.

We're all from neighbouring
villages. Shared the same school.
I see, a few chairs further down,
girls I once kissed on summer evenings.
There's one old widow, her mind long gone,
who I nearly married, until a Teddy Boy
stole her heart: the heart that, maliciously,
refuses to stop, to let her go and join him.

They don't tell you about this when
you're a kid. They should.
Ought to be a course on it.
With a recommendation.
Eat, drink and be merry. Then,
with a bit of luck, you'll die
before you lose your looks,
your eyesight, and bladder control.

We'll be led to the dining room soon,
where we'll munch our scones
and slurp our tea, like a parody
of the street parties our parents
organised, to mark the Coronation.

There's just one thing we all need,
that would make this second childhood
bearable, as it made the first joyous.

So I've called the carer over. Here
she comes. The spitting image of
one of our schoolmistresses. I'm
going to ask her what we'd all like to:

Please, Miss, I want my mum!
Can you get her to fetch me home?

Inside Out

Making the most of a colonoscopy!

The screen shows, as if in
an Attenborough documentary,
the strange, unseen world that's
an integral part of me
yet permanently out of sight.

Those coils, these intricately delicate veins,
like the colouring on some hitherto
undiscovered sea creature,
these many-ridged tunnels
are as unexpectedly elegant
as the Victorian sewers
whose brick-built avenues,
with their fabulously-tiled and
brass-adorned pumping stations
perform the same basic function
for Londoners as this fleshy concertina
does for me.

Here on the endoscopy floor, in a warm, hygienic room,
the consultant seeks to remove anything untoward,
just as weeds and saplings must be torn out
from walls and terraces before they grow
into the structures' nemesis and bring them down.

A polyp, spotted, is sliced off with the
surgical precision of an airstrike,
though one with no collateral damage

beyond a sudden smear of bright red blood
that splashes across the screen like
some vivid modernist painting.

A final check, then I am wheeled back into Recovery,
where the bright blue socks,
backless shorts (no doubt available,
for other purposes, online) and gown
are gratefully cast off and
I'm clothed and combed into the outward me,
my internal pumping station
having a brief pause before resuming
its life-long duties...

Unexpected Rapture

Earth. Mother Nature. Gaia.
They have all sorts of names for her,
but none know the secret,
sacred one she calls herself
as she performs her stately,
life-giving orbit of the sun.

Her maternal feelings for
the most advanced of her children
express themselves
through a natural abundance,
for she's enjoyed watching
humanity evolve, developing
far beyond even her beloved
whales and dolphins;
speaking across continents
on radio waves, or through
fibre optic cables laid on ocean floors,
let alone turning sand and metal ores
into spaceships.

Now, however, they've gone too far,
as plastic and pollution soil
her handiwork and choke the
very waters from which all life emerged.

Her final warning shot,
the Covid crisis,
having been ignored, she unleashes
the hurricane that sweeps

all humankind into space,
each individual bursting into flames
as they hurtle through the atmosphere's
outer edge, reduced to dust floating
in the infinite dark and cold
of an interstellar wilderness.

She took the idea from one of the most
dramatic dreams of any major religion;
the concept of a mass ascension into heaven
at the end of time and history.

Yes, she thinks, as trees and plants
seed themselves in empty streets,
while sheep come down from the hills
to claim the silent suburbs
- the meek at last inheriting the earth -
the cleansing is more than a pleasure;
it is a long-awaited Rapture.

Pillow Talk

In Peter Jones,
Sloane Square's gateway to heaven,
I'm looking for a new duvet cover,
when I spot a young man,
boy-band cute with the
obligatory floppy hair,
testing a pillow.

He holds it up to his face,
(*hold me! hold me instead!*)
which he turns sideways
so that he greets
the potential bedmate
with his cheek snuggling into
the goose down.

After a while,
having tried both sides
(*I bet you have! try mine*)
he makes his decision
and heads towards
the check-out counter
(*don't go! don't go!*)
pulling a card
from a wallet tucked
into the back pocket
of his tight-fitting trousers.
(*not jeans… so classy. I want you!*)

I watch as he heads
towards the exit,
the *joie de vivre* of
King's Road, Chelsea,
and the rest of his life
(*share mine! share mine!*)
before I pay cash for the cover
and head home, alone,
via South Kensington
tube station, from whose platform
I can see the windows
of the flat I once lived in,
where he and I might
have slept together, had
we both been then the age
he is now...
(*too old! I know! goodbye!*)

Tom Erhardt Plus One

Tom Erhardt, an American, was for many years the doyen of West End literary theatre agents, having worked for the legendary Peggy Ramsay and inheriting her clients after her death. Tall, heavily built, popular and immensely knowledgable, he was an unmissable presence at West End premieres - especially if you happened to be between him and his seat.

He was always there,
outside the theatre, ahead of time.
As was I, knowing his
penchant for punctuality,
yet, despite this, his greeting
to me was often the same:
'I thought you weren't coming!'

This reflected more a fear
of missing something on stage
than any suspicion of his
guest's unreliability. For
the stage was his life,
a platform for the performance
of his writers' work:
the stable of thoroughbreds
whose interests he represented
across the globe.

He'd march purposefully
along the stalls row,
me following in his wake,
with an unstoppable momentum
that took no notice of people's knees

58

or feet, or briefcases,
his satchel swinging at his side
like the flanking movement
of cavalry in support of the
main infantry attack as he
forced his way towards our seats.

Afterwards, in a nearby restaurant
of the old-fashioned family-run sort
he'd frequented since his arrival
in London from the States in the '60s,
his face would shine with a mixture
of Prosecco and pride in the
achievement of whichever
of his clients he had come to
see that evening.

The stroke that felled him shortly
after he retired, at 86, should
have taken him straight to some
theatrical Valhalla, a heavenly
Joe Allen's and a reunion
with Peggy Ramsay,
instead of condemning him to
five bed-bound years
made bearable only by
his many friends and a
flow of gossip…

His final curtain call was at
Golders Green, his coffin
brought in to the *Sound of
Music* - the processional

march from Maria's wedding
to Captain von Trapp.

If, on leaving this life,
we really do arrive in another,
better one, then I look
forward to being greeted
outside the pearly gates
by a smiling Tom, saying
as he moves forward for
one of his trademark hugs,
'I thought you weren't coming!'

The Death Of Lord Kitchener

Field Marshal Earl Kitchener was famous for defeating the Dervish army in the Sudan in 1898 and for his recruiting poster at the start of the First World War. He sailed from the Grand Fleet's naval base at Scapa Flow, Orkney, on the evening of 5th June, 1916, heading for Russia, at whose General Staff headquarters Tsar Nicholas II had taken personal command of the army. Both the Tsar and the British government expected the Field Marshal's presence, advice and expertise to be a major support to the Russian war effort. HMS Hampshire, the warship he was sailing on, hit a German mine and sank, drowning the great majority of those on board, including Kitchener.

He feels the explosion as much as hears it.

He and his *aide-de-camp* put on their greatcoats
and make their way to the deck,
where men are rushing around
amid the noise and flames.
One of the younger one gives him
a cheeky smile and thumbs-up
as he rushes past,
but the ship is battling a Force 9 gale
on top of the mine's havoc,
so he knows it's doomed.

Knows, too, that, given the height
of the waves, his own life is already lost,
even as he accepts a cigarette,
as if at a party, or unwinding
after inspecting a parade
of new recruits, cupping his large,

strong hands around the tiny flame
as a junior officer lights it: an act
of defiance against the storm;
a moment of calm amid
the emergency.

So, this is how it will all end.

A far cry from the desert
in which he won an enduring fame;
the heat that he loves.

He thinks of the mansion he's
bought in Egypt, a country whose
language, to people's surprise,
he speaks fluently. It's his refuge
from the English winters,
the cold and rain, the thick smog
that takes the lives of so many
men his age each year.

Ironic that it is, instead,
an English summer that has
sealed his fate.

These savage North Sea waters
slamming into the warship couldn't be
more different from the timeless
tranquility, the soothing, smooth
procession of the life-giving Nile,
beside which he and his closest
staff (he's never been much
of a one for female company)

have long, *alfresco* dinners
under the ancient star-filled sky.

As he looks around, he takes
not exactly comfort,
more a sort of bucking-up, from
another disaster at sea:
the reports he'd read
of the heroic actions of
passengers on the *Titanic*.

Business tycoons, and the musicians
who played for them as the great
liner went down, died like
gentlemen. So will he...
Pleased to have a plan of action,
he summons the young lieutenant
whose hobby he's observed
with some amusement.

'Osborne!'

'Sir?'

'How about some music to take
our minds off this temporary
unpleasantness?'

'Sir!' He pulls the harmonica
from his overcoat pocket
with a shy smile.

'A hymn, Sir?'

'Good God, no! Something cheerful!'

'Righty-ho.'

As Osborne raises the harmonica to
his mouth the ship lists
jarringly to the side, sending the
whole group tumbling into
the pitiless waves.

Kitchener feels an instant, involuntary
panic as the sea closes over him,
darkness smothers the light,
sea water fills his lungs when he struggles
to breathe and the cold,
as stunning as a sudden blow,
puts his body, despite the uniform,
the boots and the greatcoat,
into a state of shock.

Not only don't they keep him warm,
they drag him down, as they do his
companions, each one now not part
of a military unit but a desperate
individual, entirely wrapped up in
their own hopeless fight for survival,
aware of nothing but the searing
pain in their chests, the desperate
punching of their hearts against
their ribs, as if, having given up on
the bodies they have powered for
so long, they are trying to find

their own escape, their own
way to the surface.

Before he loses consciousness
and his life, Kitchener has a moment of
unexpected peace. His career doesn't
flash before his eyes, but he does
see his Egyptian house, the oasis
to which he was already sailing
when war was declared and he was
called back to London.

As his mind takes him through the
large airy rooms then out past
the cloisters towards the lawns
and ornamental ponds, he wishes
he'd had a few more winters
there, more time to see the gardens
where he...

Nothing. No thoughts. Oblivion...

At that moment, unknown to him,
as is everything now, the ship's ammunition
explodes in a fusillade of shells:
a graveside salute that also confirms
the extinction of the last hope
of a distant Tsar to rally his armies
and avoid the revolution that will take
his own life, and that of his family,
in a deafening blaze of gunfire in
a basement in Ekaterinburg...

A House In France

(A poem for Craig)

A house in France, clinging to the side
of a steep hill that slopes down
to an orchard and to woods beyond,
was left a wreck by time,
its roof long absent and
a tree growing
from the stone-flagged floor
past the 18th century chimney
and up to the sky.

His hands, able to carve, to mend,
to support, to strengthen,
took down the tree,
rebuilt the walls
and created a new roof,
a new shelter,
a fresh start for the house
and for the family,
now possessing a home
in France -
a 21st century version
of those that generations
of English knights
inhabited there in the Hundred Years War.

A quick, cruel illness and he has gone,
returned to the earth from which we've
all come,

no more visible or tangible now
than the tree he felled.
Yet, unlike that tree,
though fallen, he remains at the heart of the house,
the skill of his hands and the sweat of his brow
having created a lasting legacy
that will continue to shelter
the family he loved; his wife,
the children and grandchildren,
friends and neighbours,
whose summer shade and
winter warmth will be his gift,
until they, we, meet our end too,
transformed from living beings
into memories, stored
in the very stones,
the trees, the grass,
the nearby vines
of the house that
Craig and Carol saved
and made their own.

Taking Mother To The Hairdresser's

Taking Mother to the hairdresser,
a highlight of her widowed week.

It should be an unalloyed enjoyment for her,
and a virtue kick for me, getting her
to this sanctuary.

But she cavils and complains
from the house to the high street,
our relationship long since frayed
despite the closeness we
once enjoyed.

A duty then, instead of a pleasure,
especially when I overhear her
tell the hairdresser how much she prefers
my brother to me,
the last time we came in.

Yet, on today's visit,
as the young receptionists
give a tight little smile of greeting,
pursed lips barely hiding their disdain
for this wrinkled old woman
for whom everything is a fuss
and nothing ever quite right,
I want to shout, as her son,
that at their age she'd been beautiful.

To throw on their desk
a photo of her in her youth,
dark-haired, dark-eyed,
like a 1940s film star,
her face radiating a
casual confidence in
her sexuality
as her arm holds back
her abundant, glossy hair,
so different from the tight
bottle-coloured curls
that are teased into shape
every Tuesday.

Beautiful. Fertile. Kind.

A woman. A lover. A mother.

Instead, bitter on her behalf
at the changes of the years,
her face now more
W H Auden than
Margaret Lockwood,
I hand her over to
the young women who,
through no fault of their own,
constrained by their youth,
cannot imagine her as anything other,
or greater, than her current self.
Then, as she dismisses me
with an automatic and unfelt
'Thank you, dear',
I head off to a local café,

for a coffee and a newspaper,
'til the hour is over and I take her home
to daytime TV and a loneliness
that would have been inconceivable
when she crewed yachts
or dazzled on the dance floor,
sixty years before.